The God Really Loves You Book Series™ Presents:

GOD Really Loves You
and
He Made Everything!

**Written and Illustrated
by Wendy Nelson**

God Really Loves You Book Series™ presents:

GOD Really Loves You
and He Made Everything!

Text Copyright ©2018 by Wendy Nelson
Artwork Copyright ©2018 by Wendy Nelson

Published by MediaTek Grafx
POB 62, Bonnieville, Kentucky, 42713

ISBN 978-0-692-16738-0

Design and production by MediaTek Grafx, Bonnieville, Kentucky.

The Publisher has made every effort to avoid errors or omissions. Opinions, stories, and themes are intended for entertainment, motivation for research and future study. This book includes content that is non-fiction.

All Scripture quotations are from the The Holy Bible, King James Version, Pradis Software Rel 02.04.03, Built with Conform Version 5.00.0051, Version 5.1.50 Copyright ©2002 The Zondervan Corporation All Rights Reserved.

All rights reserved. This Publication may not be reproduced in whole or in part, stored or transmitted by any means. Media may use small portions for reviews. Please request written permission from Publisher for any other reason.

Printed in the United States of America

A Special Gift for

_____

From

_____

Note

_____
_____
_____

Date

_____

God is our Father in Heaven.
He loves everyone very much!

He loves you this much!

This much
is a whole bunch!

1 John 4:19
We love him, because he first loved us.

God made the heaven above.
God made the earth we live on.

*Genesis 1:1 In the beginning
God created the heaven and the earth.*

God made the big sun to give us light in the day.
We love sunshine!

God gave us the little moon to give us light
in the night! He made the stars, too!

Genesis 1:16 And God made two great lights; the greater light to rule the day, and the lesser light to rule the night: he made the stars also.

God made grass and trees.

He made apples and oranges and bananas, too!

Genesis 1:12 And the earth brought forth grass, and herb yielding seed after his kind, and the tree yielding fruit, whose seed was in itself, after his kind: and God saw that it was good.

God said everything was good!
God made fish and birds, too!

God made great big whales!

Genesis 1:21 And God created great whales, and every living creature that moveth, which the waters brought forth abundantly, after their kind, and every winged fowl after his kind: and God saw that it was good.

God made cows and He made lizards.

God made puppy dogs. We love animals!

Genesis 1:25 And God made the beast of the earth after his kind, and cattle after their kind, and every thing that creepeth upon the earth after his kind: and God saw that it was good.

God made man
and God made woman.

He blessed them!

*Genesis 1:27-28 So God created man
in his own image, in the image of God created he him;
male and female created he them.
And God blessed them,*

God gave animals and birds
food to eat.
God gave mommies and daddies food to eat.
God said that all was very good!

*Gensis 1:30 And to every beast of the earth,
and to every fowl of the air, and to every thing that
creepeth upon the earth, wherein there is life, I have
given every green herb for meat: and it was so.*

God is our Father in Heaven.
He loves us all very much!

*Proverbs 8:17 I love them that love me;
and those that seek me early
shall find me.*

Thank you, God,
for each new day!

Thank you, God,
for watching over us!

Psalm 36:7 How excellent is thy lovingkindness, O God! therefore the children of men put their trust under the shadow of thy wings.

God really loves you and He made everything!
Thank you, God!

God Really Loves You Book Series™

GodReallyLovesYou.com

*Proverbs 22:6 Train up a child
in the way he should go: and when he is old,
he will not depart from it.*

*Matthew 18:3-5 And said, Verily I say unto you,
Except ye be converted, and become as little children,
ye shall not enter into the kingdom of heaven.
Whosoever therefore shall humble himself
as this little child, the same is greatest in the kingdom
of heaven. And whoso shall receive
one such little child in my name receiveth me.*